50 REFRESHING,
HEALTHY, HOMEMADE
THIRST QUENCHERS

COOL
WATERS

BRIAN PRESTON-CAMPBELL

PHOTOGRAPHS BY JERRY ERRICO

THE HARVARD COMMON PRESS

Boston, Massachusetts

For Shade, a velvet, cool drink of water
—J.E.

For Rebecca, Ian, and Caleb
—B.P.-C.

The Harvard Common Press
535 Albany Street
Boston, Massachusetts 02118
www.harvardcommonpress.com

Printed in China
Printed on acid-free paper

Library of Congress Cataloging-in-Publication Data

Preston-Campbell, Brian.
   Cool waters : 50 refreshing, healthy, homemade thirst quenchers /
   Brian Preston-Campbell ; photographs by Jerry Errico.
     p. cm.
   Includes index.
    ISBN 978-1-55832-384-1 (hardcover : alk. paper)
   1. Beverages. 2. Drinking water. 3. Fruit drinks. I. Title.
TX815.P74 2009
641.2'6--dc22

                              2008022600

Special bulk-order discounts are available on this and other Harvard
Common Press books. Companies and organizations may purchase
books for premiums or resale, or may arrange a custom edition, by
contacting the Marketing Director at the address above.

Book design by Vivian Ghazarian
Photographs by Jerry Errico
Food styling by Brian Preston-Campbell
Prop styling by Martha Bernabe

Front jacket recipe: Pineapple and Lime Seltzer, page 21

10 9 8 7 6 5 4 3 2 1

Acknowledgments

Our sincere thanks to Pam Abrams, senior vice president of Downtown Bookworks, whose generosity and professional guidance brought this idea to fruition. A special thanks to Virginia Downes of The Harvard Common Press for her professionalism and enthusiasm, and for the creative freedom she engenders. Also, thank you to Martha Bernabe, stylist, whose talent and energy know no bounds.

—Jerry Errico and
Brian Preston-Campbell

Special gratitude goes to my photography agents, Tricia Scott and Brett Sahler, whose friendship I value the most.
—Jerry Errico

I extend my deepest appreciation to my editor, Valerie Cimino, and copy editor, Christine Corcoran Cox. An author only writes one first book, and I was fortunate to have two skilled and seasoned professionals to make the final stages of the process seem almost effortless. Additional gratitude goes to dietitian Cindy Sizemore for her nutritional guidance and thorough review of my recipes. And thanks to the Lower East Side Whole Foods Market, for not only stocking most of the ingredients in this book but also providing a quiet refuge in which to write it.
—Brian Preston-Campbell

Contents

Acknowledgments 3

Why Water? 6

The Basics of Flavored Water 9

Quick Quenchers 19

Nutritious Nectars 39

Special Sippers 59

Cubed Complements 79

Eau de You 92

Resources 93

Measurement Equivalents 93

Index 94

Why Water?

Water is the basis of all life on Earth, and its consumption is, without a doubt, the very foundation of a healthy lifestyle. Many knowledgeable sources, including our doctors and mothers and the mainstream media, constantly advise us to think about hydration—usually telling us to drink at least eight glasses of the clear stuff each day. While that seems like a reasonable proposal for some people, for the rest of us, there just isn't enough going on with water to make it exciting. If we are surrounded by unique food and drink experiences every day, why then does our drinking water have to be so . . . plain?

Imagine *Cool Waters* as a collection of unique cocktail recipes. But these cocktail recipes don't contain any caffeine, added sugar, excessive calories, or even alcohol. Each one is designed to be easy to prepare and, aside from a few simple exceptions, don't require any cooking. What makes the beverages in this book unique is that they are composed mostly of water, yet taste great. Each one is guaranteed to be interesting and go well with food (and other drinks as well). As a bonus, your friends and family won't know what hit them the next time they pick up a drinking glass at your house.

This imbiber's manual starts off with Quick Quenchers, recipes consisting of a few ingredients, with quick and easy steps to get you started. The basic concepts of flavoring water are covered, beginning with recipes that add a few fruit flavors, then gradually becoming more complex combinations.

Interested in an alternative to that sugary sports drink you've been using to "enhance" your workout? The recipes in Nutritious Nectars will get you started in the right direction. This chapter features many exciting ingredients, including trendy dried berries and exotic tropical fruits.

In the chapter that follows, Special Sippers, things get a lot more interesting. We travel the globe for inspiration and discover what can only be described as fusion infusions. Procuring a few of the ingredients may take slightly more effort, but the extra work will be rewarded. I promise you flavor experiences not found in any bottled beverage anywhere!

Prefer your liquids on the rocks? Your chance will come with the unique ice cube recipes found in Cubed Complements. Forget about plain old ice and throw some of these frozen flavors in your glass. They're also a convenient way to spice up plain old flavorless water—keep a few varieties in the freezer for whenever the mood strikes you.

Just how many possible flavors of water could one make? It seems that the combinations are endless—limited only by your creativity and access to unique ingredients. Eau de You, at the back of the book, is devoted to the creation of your own signature flavored water. Feel free to experiment with the ingredients listed in whatever combinations appeal to you most. Cheers!

The Basics of Flavored Water

BE STILL

Much of the water needed for the recipes in this book is still, simply meaning it is H_2O without bubbles. The water from your faucet is the least expensive, most environmentally responsible choice, and often it is the best source. If you are like me and find your municipal tap water has an acceptable, neutral flavor, then it's ideal for these recipes. Don't have good-tasting tap water? No problem—there are several options to move your water in the right direction. Special pitchers from several companies, including Brita, PŪR, and Culligan, are a convenient way to keep a couple of liters of filtered drinking water cold in your refrigerator. The filters on these pitchers can be a little slow, however, especially when the pitcher is empty and you're ready to infuse water now.

For instant gratification, PŪR, Brita, Waterpik, and several other companies make filters that fit right on the end of your kitchen faucet. The threaded couplers screw onto your existing hardware, allowing you to enjoy filtered water with almost no effort and at a faster flow rate than filtered pitchers—½ gallon per minute for faucet filters, compared to ½ cup per minute for pitchers. Faucet filters all have a switch to allow regular tap water to flow when you don't need to use filtered—for washing pots and pans, for example. Many also include an indicator that will inform you when the filter needs to be changed—about every three months or 120 gallons in most cases, but your mileage may vary depending upon how much water you consume and how many people in your house use the filter.

A similar option to the faucet filter is the countertop filter. These appliances are made by several enterprising companies, including Aquasana, Multi-Pure, and Doulton. Much like the faucet filters, countertop filters have a coupler that attaches directly to the faucet. The coupler is attached to one or two flexible tubes that connect to the main body of the filter. This is where the filtration occurs, and in most cases, where the water is dispensed (some divert the water back to a spout just under the sink faucet). There is a small valve and a specialized spout from which the clean water is drawn for consumption. The upside to this piece of equipment is that the filters are much larger than the two previously mentioned solutions and they don't require a plumber (or in some cases, any tools whatsoever) for installation. The downside to this option is that the filter takes up precious countertop space. Expect to pay more, as well, for this type of filter.

For many of us, the most accessible alternative to tap water is bottled water. However, in these environmentally conscious times, bottled-water producers are taking a lot of heat from green-minded consumers. More than 8 billion gallons of bottled water are used annually in the United States for drinking water, and many of the bottles holding that drinking water will go unrecycled, straight into a landfill. Additionally, the average price of an ounce of bottled water is higher than the average price of an ounce of gasoline in the United States. With all of that said, there remains a large demand for bottled water. It might be the best choice for your personal consumption—you may believe that your tap water contains too many chemicals or heavy metals for your family to consume safely. Your tap water may taste strongly of chlorine, a common sanitizing agent added by water authorities the world over. Or it may be either too hard or soft for your preferences. Whatever the reason, the type of water you consume is a personal choice. If possible, purchase your water in glass bottles—glass is more easily recycled than plastic. Glass bottles can also be refilled easily with the flavored water you make, so try to reuse before recycling whenever possible.

BUBBLES EVERYWHERE

I like to think of this book as a do-it-yourself water manual. Filter it, flavor it, drink it, chill it—simple enough for recipes using still water, right? But what about the recipes that call for sparkling water? With the right equipment, making those recipes is just as simple. Depending on your needs and budget, there are three options for making your own carbonated water.

Whatever you may call your sparkling water—fizzy water, soda water, club soda, seltzer, or pop water—they are all the same basic thing: water with the addition of carbon dioxide gas (CO_2). The CO_2 is dissolved in the water and creates a solution that is called carbonic acid (H_2CO_3). As a Pennsylvanian transplanted to New York City in my early twenties, I vacillate between the terms "soda water" and "seltzer," but the name you choose for your sparkling water will most likely be influenced by where you grew up or currently live. For the purposes of the recipes that call for it, we'll simply refer to it as "sparkling water."

The first, and least expensive, option for bubbly-water production is the soda siphon. It also yields the smallest overall quantities of water with the least control over the amount of carbonation in the finished product. The soda siphon consists of nothing more than a metal bottle with a dispenser at the top, a small cartridge of CO_2, and a means to inject the gas into the water. There are a couple of commonly available models, a 1-liter bottle from iSi North America and a 2-liter bottle from Liss. Both use the same steel cylinders of CO_2 to charge the water, and they are widely available as well. Look for the bottles and gas (usually located near one another) in housewares stores or the kitchen department of big-box retailers. (See the Resources section, page 93, for online sources.) Using these bottles is as simple as filling them with the water of your choice and then screwing on the CO_2 cartridge to charge the bottle. I have found that the bubbles are the least prominent when using the water immediately after charging, but after a few hours in the fridge the situation improves considerably. After chilling, the water has much larger, more numerous bubbles. I've found these bottles to be the best choice for those who do not wish to make a large initial investment, and for those lacking the storage space for one of the larger options discussed below. The good environmental news is that the steel cylinders containing the CO_2 are recyclable in most areas that take mixed metals.

The second in-home option for making sparkling water is the line of countertop machines from a company called Soda-Club. It offers three models, the Fountain Jet and Edition 1, which are basically the same with only cosmetic differences, and the larger and more expensive Penguin. The Fountain Jet and Edition 1 (about $100) can charge 1 liter of water at a time in reusable plastic bottles, while the Penguin (about $250) includes glass carafes with a smaller volume of 620 milliliters. The amount of fizz produced by all three machines is infinitely adjustable, from tiny to assertively large bubbles. The empty CO_2 cylinders are sent back to Soda-Club for refilling.

The third and most extreme option for personal fizzy-water production is Everpure's Exubera Sparkling and Chilled Water Appliance, a plumber-installed, under-cabinet model with a whopping price tag of about $3,000. Its features are attractive, however. This appliance can instantly deliver up to 6.6 gallons of carbonated water at a temperature of 40°F at the flick of a very stylish faucet. Each $100 CO_2 cylinder can make up to 30 gallons of carbonated water, and the amount of fizz is adjustable to your liking.

On the other hand, you may have the good fortune to live in an area where seltzer delivery is available. In most parts of the country, gone are the days when the seltzer man came down your block, hefting cases full of beautiful glass bottles filled with sparkling water. Some urban markets still offer regular seltzer deliveries, though, and if you live in one of those areas, you might want to give it a try. The great thing about this service is that the environmental impact is low—the bottles are reused by the soda companies for decades and work perfectly time after time. Also, the supplier is usually located a short distance from your home, reducing the greenhouse gases associated with water that has traveled hundreds or even thousands of miles to your door.

Want something a little more esoteric in your effervescent creations? Then by all means try sparkling mineral water. There are a lot of brands on the market, from the old favorites Perrier (France) and San Pellegrino (Italy) to a host of newer imports to the United States, such as Vichy Catalan (Spain), Peñafiel (Mexico), and Ty Nant (Wales). Ideally, choose a neutral-tasting water without a lot of mineral aftertaste, as this might conflict with the flavors you'll be adding. Many are available in glass bottles, which, as mentioned earlier, are much more easily recycled than plastic bottles. And if you happen to be super enviro-conscious, you can easily refill and reuse those bottles with regular or homemade flavored drinking water.

If none of these options suit your personal circumstances, the sparkling water found in your local supermarket will also fit the bill. It's certainly fizzy—so fizzy that it can burst forth when a new bottle is opened— as well as inexpensive and convenient. As with a lot of still bottled water, commercially made sparkling water is derived from filtered municipal tap water and should taste clean and sparkling. These bottles carry the same hefty environmental bill as non-bubbly bottled water, however. If you choose this option, be sure to recycle those bottles!

TOOLS

During my years working in professional kitchens, I came to realize a universal truth in cooking: Any time spent in the kitchen should be time used wisely. To this end, I have found that the best way to ensure you are working at your peak efficiency is to have the appropriate tools on hand to get the job done. The list that follows is by no means absolutely requisite or complete but is simply meant to help make your production of flavored water a quick and easy process.

● SIEVE

A fine-mesh sieve or strainer is an indispensable tool for any cook. This kitchen wonder is adept at creating velvety soups and sauces by removing the fine particles contained therein. Its ability to remove the unwanted also makes the fine-mesh sieve ideal for use with the recipes in this book. Many of the infusions require extended contact between the water and the ingredients that will give it flavor. When the time comes to remove those ingredients, however, we call in the sieve to leave us with a pleasant drinking experience—one without unexpected surprises, such as dried spice bits or whole pieces of fruit in our water.

● SACHET

There's a wonderful, time-tested technique in classical French cooking in which cheesecloth is filled with aromatic herbs, spices, and vegetables, tied with twine, and placed into a pot of cooking broth to steep. This is a very useful method for adding just the right amount of a specific flavor to a cooked dish, without the need to strain out unwanted bits of herbs and spices at the end.

Throughout this book, I employ the same principle. Think of the sachet as a custom-made tea bag, filled with exactly what your recipe calls for. Instead of cooking the sachet in a liquid and rapidly extracting flavors, however, we'll take a slow and cold approach, coaxing the character out of the sachet contents in the refrigerator. To make a sachet, cut a 12 x 12-inch piece of cheesecloth and a 12-inch piece of kitchen twine. Fold the cheesecloth in half, then in half again to make a 6 x 6-inch square. Fill the center of the square with the ingredients you wish to infuse in the water. Gather the corners of the cheesecloth, containing all of the ingredients inside, between your thumb and forefinger, hold them together tightly, and tie the sachet shut with one end of the twine. Place the sachet in your pitcher or infusing vessel and tie the long end of the twine around the pitcher's handle. This will make it easier to remove the sachet later.

● TEA BALL

We won't be making any tea with this book, but a tea ball will still come in handy. A tea ball is simply an alternative to the sachet. It comes in different styles and sizes, but only the largest tea balls will accommodate the recipes in this book. A few enterprising companies have begun to market large tea balls as "herb" balls. The great part about the tea ball is that it is reusable and ready to go whenever the need arises.

● BLENDER

The blender is an indispensable part of my kitchen. I couldn't imagine trying to make marinades, pureed soups, or vinaigrettes without one. It definitely comes in handy when making flavored water as well. For our purposes, the blender is an ideal way to reduce the large ingredients in a recipe into smaller units—smaller pieces mean faster flavor exchange and less time waiting for your infusion to reach completion.

A handheld immersion blender can be just as handy, provided the ingredients you wish to blend are small enough to fit into the blade area of the blender. If you go this route, just remember that it may be necessary to use additional liquid to achieve the same effect as with a standard countertop blender. The best feature of the hand blender, in my opinion, is how easily it can be cleaned. With far fewer parts than a standard blender, it's usually only necessary to quickly wash the stick portion.

● FOOD PROCESSOR

The food processor was perhaps the twentieth century's most significant addition to the modern cook's tool kit. It slices, chops, purees—we all know the spiel. For the recipes in this book the food processor does what a blender can't quite do—finely chop fruits or vegetables with little or no added liquid. The food processor is worth its weight in gold for that one trick alone. Try to finely mince a whole beet in a blender and you'll see what I mean. Then see how long it takes you to do it by hand.

● MORTAR AND PESTLE

An ancient set of tools that does one thing very well, the mortar and pestle are what you need when you want to pulverize. I also love it for crushing whole dried spices into more reasonable sizes. The next best thing? Use a heavy saucepan to crush your spices on a clean cutting board.

● MUDDLER

A muddler is just a long pestle, repurposed for use in the creation of cocktails. It is simple to operate: Get a muddler, a tall drinking glass, and

some fruit. Throw the fruit in the bottom of the glass, mash it with the muddler, add liquid, and stir. For many of the recipes in this book a muddler will be quite handy, particularly if you have a large quantity of fruit to mash.

● PITCHERS AND STIR RODS

Throughout this book, practically every recipe mentions employing at least one large pitcher (and often two) to hold your beverages throughout the prep process. Ideally, the pitcher you choose should hold a half gallon (or 2 liters) to accommodate all of the ingredients, both liquid and solid. Drink a lot of flavored water and you may find yourself needing three or more such pitchers. Fortunately, there are plenty of inexpensive pitchers to be found—an investment that will prove useful for a myriad of drinks, not just flavored water.

You'll need something to stir the water in your pitcher(s), and it should be long enough to reach the bottom. While stir rods aren't necessary, they do bring a higher level of sophistication to your water presentation. A simple wooden spoon will do fine, but if you have a long glass rod at your disposal, by all means use it whenever you feel the need to show off.

ON ICE

Hypothetical situation: You're throwing a party and you want to make three of the Cubed Complements recipes (page 79). Each recipe requires two ice cube trays, but you only have four. This leaves you with two choices: Either buy more ice cube trays (they are pretty inexpensive, after all, but you may find yourself too busy to run out for one more thing), or freeze a recipe, bag the cubes in a gallon-size freezer bag, and then reuse the trays to continue with the other recipes. Problem solved. This is also a great way to make cubes ahead and hold them for long-term storage. Just don't forget to label the cubes or you could end up putting Strawberry-Kiwi Cubes (page 87) in your Tomato Essence with Horseradish and Cucumber (page 60), and that may not give you the refreshing experience you were hoping for.

PORTABILITY

At some point you may have the need to transport your water. Unless your pitcher has a tight-fitting lid, moving more than a liter of water a long distance can be a messy prospect. Save a few plastic, glass, or aluminum jugs with lids for just such a purpose. Or reduce your guilt about buying all those 1- and 2-liter bottles of seltzer, refill them with your completed water recipe, screw on the cap, and go. If you want your water to be cold when you arrive at your destination, put the water in the jug and place it in the freezer for an hour, then put on the lid, and store it in a cooler. Surround it with a couple of bags of Cubed Complements (page 79) or plain ice and you're off.

HOW LONG WILL IT KEEP?

All of the finished recipes in this book need to be refrigerated, as most contain perishable ingredients. Fruits and vegetables add naturally occurring sugars that are absolutely irresistible to microbes if left at room temperature. None of the flavored waters should be kept longer than 3 days in the fridge, to ensure that the flavors are fresh and lively and that the majority of the nutrients remain intact.

Be sure to wash all fruits, vegetables, and herbs thoroughly before using them in any of these recipes. Taking this extra step will remove many of the germs and bacteria found on the surfaces of your produce, and the resulting water will last longer in the refrigerator, taste better, and provide the maximum health benefits to your body.

Quick Quenchers

Can you imagine an ingredient that is more neutral tasting than water? Add in a couple of flavorful components and your everyday tap water transcends mere hydration. I assure you that this is anything but a new concept—people have been enjoying a simple slice of citrus in their water glasses for centuries. But why stop there? Here are 14 quick and easy H_2O enhancers.

Squirt of Citrus	**Crimson Dew**
Pineapple and Lime Seltzer	**Sweet Tart**
Honeydew-Mint Mist	**Lychee and Lime Water**
Sparkling Meyer Lemon Water	**Clean Spearmint Water**
Rose Water with Lemon	**Mora Picante**
Blueberry Twist	**June Fields**
Red Cherry Spritzer	**Mango-Ginger "Beer"**

SQUIRT OF CITRUS

Four citrus varieties bring this water alive with freshness and vitamin C. A tall glass in the early morning is a great way to start your day. The best results come from the freshest fruits—pasteurized juice or juice from concentrate won't cut it here. But the fresh fruit quantities needed are small, so it will take only a minute or two for squeezing.

1 orange, such as navel
1 lime
1 lemon
1 ruby red grapefruit
6 cups still water
Ice cubes (optional)

1. Cut all the fruit in half and squeeze the juices into a 2-cup measuring cup.
2. Pour all the juice through a fine-mesh strainer into a large pitcher. (You may skip this step if you prefer a small amount of pulp in your water.)
3. Add the water, stir, and serve over ice, if desired.

5 MINUTES

6 SERVINGS

FOOD PAIRINGS: Mediterranean food, omelets and other egg dishes

TIP: Use a citrus reamer to make short work of juicing the fruit.

PINEAPPLE AND LIME SELTZER

The subtle black pepper flavor in this water adds an unexpected twist—yet it matches perfectly with the pineapple and lime flavors. Be sure to use the freshest pineapple you can find—a leaf from the center of the pineapple crown should be easy to remove when the fruit is ready to be consumed. Avoid pineapples with soft spots or a dark-colored bottom.

2 limes
1 cup still water
1 cup finely diced fresh pineapple
10 black peppercorns, crushed
4 cups chilled sparkling water
Ice cubes

1. Juice the limes into a pitcher, reserving the juiced halves. Add the still water.
2. Place the pineapple, peppercorns, and lime halves in a sachet (page 14). Place the sachet in the pitcher and tie the remaining twine onto the handle. Allow to steep for at least 2 hours.
3. Remove the sachet, squeezing any liquid that remains inside back into the pitcher. Add the sparkling water and stir. Serve over ice.

10 MINUTES
+
2 hours to steep

4 SERVINGS

FOOD PAIRINGS: Indian food, grilled fish, pork

TIP: If you don't have a mortar and pestle, you can use a clean meat mallet to crush the peppercorns (or any other spice in this book that requires crushing).

HONEYDEW-MINT MIST

This refreshing beverage is inspired by *agua de melón*, a traditional Mexican drink. I removed the white cane sugar from the original for this more healthful version. Mint adds a clean, herbal note to the sweet green flavor of the honeydew.

1 cup ripe honeydew melon chunks (about ¼ melon)
15 large, fresh mint leaves
4 cups chilled still water

1. Puree all the ingredients together in a blender.
2. Pour through a fine-mesh sieve into a large pitcher. Chill well before serving.

10 MINUTES

4 SERVINGS

FOOD PAIRINGS: Tacos, shellfish, poultry, spicy foods

TIP: To find perfectly ripe honeydew, simply smell the stem end of the fruit (this end has a bigger circular blemish, distinguishing it from the blossom end). If you smell fresh, ripe melon, then it's ready for use.

SPARKLING MEYER LEMON WATER

A classic touch for water is a simple slice or squeeze of lemon, but this tonic goes two steps further. Believed to be an orange and lemon hybrid of Chinese origin, the Meyer lemon is slightly sweeter than and just as flavorful as a regular lemon. Add it to bubbly water and the experience is practically sublime.

3 Meyer lemons (2 whole and 1 sliced)
6 cups chilled sparkling water
1 recipe Minty Cubes (optional, page 80)

1. Cut the whole lemons in half and squeeze the juice into a pitcher. (If your lemons have a lot of seeds, strain the lemon juice through a small sieve into the pitcher.) Add the lemon halves to the pitcher.
2. Pour in the water and Minty Cubes, if desired, and stir.
3. Garnish with the sliced lemons and serve cold.

5 MINUTES

6 SERVINGS

FOOD PAIRINGS: Salads, poultry, seafood

TIP: Feel free to substitute Grape Cubes (page 83) for the Minty Cubes. Kids love the lemon-grape combination.

ROSE WATER WITH LEMON

Imagine drinking the flavor of roses, perfectly balanced with the tartness of lemon and the sweetness of fennel seed. Rose water has been popular in the cuisines of southern and western Asia and the Middle East for centuries.

3 fennel seeds, crushed
4 cups chilled still water
Juice of 1 lemon
4 tablespoons rose water
Ice cubes

1. Put the fennel seeds in a small pan with ¼ cup of the water and bring to a simmer. Turn off the heat and allow to cool.
2. Pour the remaining still water into a large pitcher, and add the lemon juice and rose water.
3. Strain the fennel infusion into the pitcher, stir, and serve over ice.

10 MINUTES

4 SERVINGS

FOOD PAIRINGS: Salads, light seafood dishes, pastries

TIP: Look for rose water in Middle Eastern and specialty grocers and large supermarkets. Never use roses from your local florist to make your own rose water, as commercially grown flowers are heavily treated with pesticides and fertilizers.

BLUEBERRY TWIST

Blueberry and lemon are two flavors that were practically made to go together. I've seen so many recipes that wed the two that to see blueberries listed without some form of lemon seems almost unorthodox. The ginger gives a little kick of spice at the end, a surprise finish that will leave your friends guessing when they taste it.

½ cup fresh blueberries
Zest of ½ lemon
1 large pinch of ground ginger
1 cup still water
4 cups chilled sparkling water

1. Place the blueberries, lemon zest, ginger, and still water in a blender. Blend on high speed until smooth, for about 1 minute. Strain through a fine-mesh sieve into a large pitcher.
2. Add the sparkling water, stir gently, and serve.

5 MINUTES

4 SERVINGS

FOOD PAIRINGS: Red meat and game, shepherd's pie

TIP: Serve with Charentais Melon and Fennel Cubes (page 88) for an added flavor bonus.

RED CHERRY SPRITZER

This spritzer is a sure favorite of both kids and adults; the subtle cinnamon flavor makes this drink taste almost like cherry pie. Use fresh cherries at the peak of season; look for blemish-free fruit with a lot of color. In a pinch, frozen cherries can be used in this recipe, but please don't entertain the idea of using maraschino cherries!

1 cup fresh cherries, pitted and finely chopped
One 4-inch cinnamon stick, crushed
1 cup still water
4 cups chilled sparkling water
Ice cubes

1. Place the cherries, cinnamon, and still water in a blender. Blend on high speed until smooth, for about 1 minute.
2. Strain through a fine-mesh sieve into a large pitcher. Add the sparkling water and stir. Serve over ice.

10 MINUTES

5 SERVINGS

FOOD PAIRINGS: Roast beef sandwiches, grilled tuna

TIP: Use a cherry/olive pitter to make quick work of pit removal.

CRIMSON DEW

This simple recipe brings ingredients from two corners of the world together—lemongrass from Southeast Asia and blood oranges from the Mediterranean. Look for blood oranges in your market from November to May. There are several popular varieties, including the Sanguinello, the Moro, and the Tarocco. The color in blood oranges occurs naturally, affected by factors including sunlight, temperature, and the variety of the orange.

4 stalks lemongrass
Juice of 2 blood oranges
4 cups still water

1. Peel the outer layers from the lemongrass stalks and discard. Cut the stalks into 2-inch pieces and crush with a heavy knife. Tie the lemongrass into a bundle with kitchen twine.

2. Place the orange juice and water in a large pitcher. Add the lemongrass bundle and let steep in the refrigerator for at least 2 hours. Remove the lemongrass and serve cold.

10

MINUTES
+
2 hours
to steep

4

SERVINGS

FOOD PAIRINGS: Thai food, empanadas, mild fish

TIP: Look for fresh lemongrass in Asian markets in your area. Any extra stalks easily take root after a week or two in a jar of water and, when potted, they grow quickly in warm climates.

SWEET TART

This drink is subtly sweet, mildly tart, and definitely refreshing. I try to use fresh cranberries throughout the fall and winter whenever I make this recipe, but frozen berries work just fine the rest of the year.

½ cup fresh or frozen cranberries, plus more for garnish
1 large Red Delicious apple, cored and coarsely chopped
1 tablespoon freshly squeezed lemon juice
1 small pinch of ground nutmeg
6 cups chilled still water

1. Place the cranberries, apple, lemon juice, nutmeg, and 2 cups of the water in a blender. Blend on high speed until smooth, for about 1 minute. Strain through a fine-mesh sieve into a large pitcher.
2. Add the remaining water and stir gently. Garnish the glasses with a few additional whole cranberries. They float!

5 MINUTES

6 SERVINGS

FOOD PAIRINGS: Great with a Thanksgiving feast or just about any other cold-weather occasion

TIP: I buy extra bags of fresh cranberries in the fall, when they are abundant and inexpensive, and freeze them for later use.

LYCHEE AND LIME WATER

Native to southern China, lychees are now grown domestically in Hawaii, California, and Florida. This fruit is best eaten as close to the time of harvest as possible, as they begin to deteriorate quickly—look for lychees with light to medium red, blemish-free shells. You will likely find them at Asian grocers or in Chinatowns.

10 fresh lychees, peeled and seeded
Juice of 2 limes
1 teaspoon orange blossom water
6 cups chilled still water

1. Place the lychees, lime juice, orange blossom water, and 2 cups of the still water in a blender. Blend on high speed until smooth, for about 2 minutes. Strain through a fine-mesh sieve into a large pitcher.
2. Add the remaining still water, stir gently, and serve.

10 MINUTES

6 SERVINGS

FOOD PAIRINGS: Practically any variety of Asian food goes well with this unique beverage.

TIP: Fresh lychees can be hard to come by, even during the fruit's season from July to October. If you cannot locate fresh lychees, you may use canned lychees, but be sure to drain and rinse them well, as they usually come packed in a heavy sugar syrup.

CLEAN SPEARMINT WATER

This is perhaps the simplest, yet most refreshing, drink in the book. Pair with Minty Cubes (page 80) for a double mint whammy, or with Orange Blossom and Vanilla Cubes (page 85) for an additional flavor layer. The key to extracting a clean mint flavor is allowing this infusion to develop overnight in the fridge—don't try to rush the process by adding heat, or you'll only end up making mint tea and destroying most of the fresh green flavor as a result.

8 cups still water
2 large bunches fresh spearmint

1. Pour the water into a large pitcher. Gather the mint in your hands and crush it into a ball. This will release a lot more flavor from the mint (and make your hands smell great!).
2. Place the mint in the water and refrigerate overnight. There is no need to strain the water before serving, but if you wish, you can remove the larger mint stems and leaves with a slotted spoon. Serve cold.

5 MINUTES + overnight to steep

6 SERVINGS

FOOD PAIRINGS: Thanks to its clean, refreshing flavor, this water complements all foods.

TIP: Mint is an easy herb to grow—it thrives with little care and spreads quickly. The best mint is freshly cut and used soon after harvest.

MORA PICANTE

Mora means "blackberry" in Spanish, and *picante* denotes sharp or spicy flavor. The ancho chile in this recipe gives the water an unexpected kick and a full flavor without adding a mouth-burning spiciness. Be sure not to substitute regular chili powder for the ground ancho chile, as most commercial chili powders contain cumin, oregano, and a few other flavors you probably don't want in your water.

15 fresh blackberries
1½ teaspoons ground ancho chile
1 teaspoon ground cinnamon
4 cups still water
Ice cubes

1. Muddle the blackberries, ancho chile, cinnamon, and ½ cup of the water in a glass measuring cup for at least 1 minute.
2. With a ladle, wooden spoon, or rubber spatula, force the mixture through a fine-mesh sieve into a large pitcher. Add the remaining water and allow to rest for 15 minutes in the refrigerator.
3. Serve the water over ice (or try Tangerine-Ginger Cubes, page 81).

20
MINUTES

4
SERVINGS

FOOD PAIRINGS:
Mexican or any Latin American food

TIP: If you are unable to find ground ancho chile, look for dried whole ancho chiles. Remove the stems and seeds and grind them with a mortar and pestle or in an electric spice grinder.

JUNE FIELDS

I look forward to June every year in anticipation of eating as many local strawberries as I can before they disappear from the farmers' markets. Lavender brings a clean, herbaceous complement to the ripe, red fruit in this recipe, and the sparkling water is a cleansing transport for the combined flavors.

1 cup fresh strawberries, hulled
1 cup still water
1 teaspoon fresh lavender leaves
4 cups chilled sparkling water

1. Puree the strawberries in a blender with the still water until smooth, for about 1 minute. During the last 10 seconds, add the lavender.
2. Strain through a fine-mesh sieve into a large pitcher. Add the sparkling water, stir gently, and serve.

10 MINUTES

4 SERVINGS

FOOD PAIRINGS:
Salads, desserts

TIP: Dried lavender is not an acceptable substitute for fresh in this recipe. Look for fresh lavender in natural-food stores and in the herb section of large supermarkets.

MANGO-GINGER "BEER"

Traditional ginger beer is laden with sugar, so here's a version that uses tropical mango for natural sweetness to balance the spice from two kinds of ginger, fresh and dried. Each adds a slightly different note of ginger flavor.

1 cup diced ripe mango
One 4-inch piece unpeeled fresh ginger, coarsely chopped
1 tablespoon ground ginger
¼ teaspoon ground white pepper
1 cup still water
6 cups chilled sparkling water

1. Place the mango, fresh ginger, ground ginger, white pepper, and still water in a blender. Blend on high speed until smooth, for about 1 minute.
2. Strain through a fine-mesh sieve into a large pitcher. Add the sparkling water, stir gently, and serve.

 10 MINUTES

 6 SERVINGS

FOOD PAIRINGS: Jamaican food, of course, as well as any other Caribbean cuisine

TIP: White pepper has a milder flavor than traditional black pepper, which makes it ideal for this recipe.

Nutritious Nectars

Rehydrate and replenish trace vitamins
and minerals with a couple of glasses of these great-tasting, nutritious nectars. Get rid of those sugary sports drinks and "enhanced waters" that promise increased performance but deliver artificial flavors and colors. Reenergize in the morning or unwind at the end of the day—there's a quick solution here to suit your active lifestyle.

Green Herb Infusion

Eau de Carotte

Workout Fuel

Cucumberade

Antioxidant Power

Aloe-Asis

Inner Earth

Liquid Iron

Pure Pectin

Simply Balmy

Wet/Dry

Pomegranate Flair

Wind-Down

GREEN HERB INFUSION

Drink this herbal tonic half an hour before exercising, or have a glass with a light lunch. The three herbs in this recipe contain flavonoids, which have been shown to be beneficial for reducing cardiovascular risk. Health benefits aside, I find this to be a soothing, almost addictive tonic.

Juice of ½ lime
4 cups still water
1 tablespoon fresh parsley leaves
4 to 6 fresh peppermint leaves
2 fresh basil leaves
5 mustard seeds

1. Add the lime juice and 3 cups of the water to a large pitcher.
2. Place the parsley, peppermint, basil, and mustard seeds in a blender with the remaining 1 cup water. Puree until smooth, for about 1 minute.
3. Strain the pureed mixture through a fine-mesh sieve into the pitcher. Serve cold.

10 MINUTES

4 SERVINGS

FOOD PAIRINGS: Poached fish, grilled chicken, salads

TIP: Garnish with additional herbs and lime slices, if desired.

EAU DE CAROTTE

The fresh flavors of carrot, green apple, and fresh ginger in this drink are sure to jump-start your workout. This water is alive with the earthy tone of the beta carotene–packed carrot and a slight floral note from the apple.

1 medium-size carrot, coarsely chopped
½ Granny Smith apple, cored
One 1-inch piece unpeeled fresh ginger, grated
4 cups chilled still water

1. Place the carrot, apple, and ginger in a blender with 2 cups of the water and puree until smooth, for about 1 minute.
2. Strain the puree through a fine-mesh sieve into a large pitcher, pressing on the solids with a ladle or rubber spatula to extract as much juice as possible. Add the remaining water and stir. Serve cold.

5 MINUTES

4 SERVINGS

FOOD PAIRINGS:
Egg dishes, tuna salad

TIP: Given that the solids are strained in the end, I suggest not peeling the carrots or apples. Important nutrients reside in the outer layer of the carrot, and the apple peel adds flavor and nutrients as well—just be sure to wash them thoroughly before proceeding.

...KOUT FUEL

Drink a few glasses of this before, during, and after a strenuous workout—its taste surpasses that of any bottled sports drink, and it has far fewer calories. Coconut water is a natural electrolyte-replacing rehydrator—exactly what you need from a sports drink. Other nutrients here are vitamin C, iron, and calcium. If you cannot find golden kiwis, use green.

2 golden kiwis, peeled
One 2-inch piece fresh ginger, peeled and coarsely chopped
1 cup fresh or unsweetened canned coconut water
Pinch of sea salt
4 cups still water

2 cans
sweeter
:)

1. Place all of the ingredients in a blender and puree until smooth, for about 1 minute.
2. Strain the puree through a fine-mesh sieve into a pitcher. Serve cold or at room temperature.

5 MINUTES **4** SERVINGS

FOOD PAIRINGS:
Fish, shellfish, Japanese food

TIP: Don't confuse coconut water with coconut milk or cream of coconut. Canned coconut water can be found at many grocers and health-food stores. See the Resources section (page 93) for an online source.

CUCUMBERADE

Inspired by a trip to a spa, this simple combination of cucumber and citrus not only tastes great, it also provides electrolytes and vitamin C. Be sure to drink this water the day it is made, as the sliced cucumbers quickly lose their delicate flavor.

2 large cucumbers
Juice of 1 lemon
Juice of 1 lime
Small pinch of sea salt
6 cups still water

1. Thinly slice one of the cucumbers and reserve. Peel, seed, and coarsely chop the second cucumber.

2. Puree the chopped cucumber with the lemon and lime juices, salt, and 1 cup of the water in a blender. Strain through a fine-mesh sieve into a large pitcher, using a ladle or rubber spatula to extract as much juice from the pulp as possible.

3. Add the remaining water and the cucumber slices, stir gently, and serve. To intensify the cucumber flavor, allow the water to steep for a couple of hours in the refrigerator.

10 MINUTES

6 SERVINGS

FOOD PAIRINGS: Salads and other light fare; it also tastes great first thing in the morning with a bowl of fruit.

TIP: The skins of conventionally grown cucumbers are usually waxed to improve their shelf life. Be sure to scrub them well before use to remove as much as possible of this harmless but unnecessary preservative.

ANTIOXIDANT POWER

When was the last time your water was intense? Every ingredient in this recipe, except the water, contains high levels of antioxidants, which have been shown to prevent oxidization in the body, a naturally occurring process that can result in a number of diseases associated with aging. This water also contains vitamin A, vitamin C, iron, and calcium.

20 fresh blueberries
10 fresh blackberries
10 seedless red grapes
¼ small red beet, peeled and coarsely chopped
1 tablespoon unsweetened Dutch-processed
   cocoa powder
4 cups chilled still water

1. Puree all the ingredients in a blender until smooth, for about 1 minute.
2. Strain through a fine-mesh sieve into a pitcher. Serve cold.

10 MINUTES

4 SERVINGS

FOOD PAIRINGS:
Red meat, grilled pork

TIP: Be sure to use Dutch-processed cocoa powder in this recipe, as it is less acidic than natural cocoa.

ALOE-ASIS

Aloe vera is actually a member of the lily family (along with garlic and onions), and it originated in northern Africa. It has a long history of use as a medicinal food to treat gastric distress. Although aloe vera doesn't have much flavor of its own, its pairing here with star fruit and a little citrus juice creates a sublimely balanced beverage.

½ cup peeled and diced fresh aloe vera leaf,
   or ½ cup aloe vera juice
1 ripe carambola (star fruit)
Juice of 1 lemon
Juice of 1 orange
6 cups still water

1. Puree the aloe vera leaves or juice, carambola, and lemon and orange juice in a blender or food processor, for about 1 minute.
2. Strain through a fine-mesh sieve into a large pitcher, add the water, and stir. Serve cold or at room temperature.

15 MINUTES

6 SERVINGS

FOOD PAIRINGS: Light seafood and poultry dishes

TIP: Be sure to remove all skin and any yellow parts of the aloe leaf before use. Some people report sensitivity to the aloe sap found in these parts of the plant.

INNER EARTH

It should come as no surprise that root vegetables are usually the most nutritious—they're the parts of the plant that mingle directly with the beneficial nutrients trapped in the soil. Artificially fortified waters are the stuff of food chemists; this one contains actual vitamins and minerals from plant sources grown in real dirt.

1 large red beet, peeled
½ medium-size celery root, peeled
1 small radish (optional)
1 small carrot
Dash of soy sauce
6 cups still water

1. Coarsely chop all of the vegetables and place them in a large food processor. Puree well and transfer to a sachet (page 14). Place the sachet in a large pitcher, add the soy sauce and water, and allow to steep in the refrigerator for at least 4 hours and up to 12 hours.
2. Remove the sachet, squeezing out as much juice as possible. Stir gently and serve.

15 MINUTES
+
4 hours
to steep

6 SERVINGS

FOOD PAIRINGS: Pot roasts, stews, and other hearty winter fare

TIP: Save the beet greens—they make a great side dish sautéed with garlic in olive oil. Be sure to thoroughly wash and peel the celery root. A lot of dirt and sand get trapped in the crevices of this odd-looking vegetable.

LIQUID IRON

Leafy green vegetables are an ideal source of iron and calcium, but cooking them can destroy many of the water-soluble minerals you hope to gain from eating them. This preparation retains most of the nutrients that would otherwise be lost in the cooking process and imparts an earthy green flavor that you will surely enjoy.

2 stalks red Swiss chard, chopped
¼ cup chopped spinach leaves
¼ cup chopped purple kale
1 teaspoon loose green tea leaves
6 cups still water

1. Place the chard, spinach, kale, and tea leaves in a blender with 1 cup of the water. Puree until fairly smooth, for about 1 minute.
2. Strain through a fine-mesh sieve into a large pitcher, using a ladle or rubber spatula to extract as much juice as possible. Add the remaining water, stir gently, and serve.

15 MINUTES

6 SERVINGS

FOOD PAIRINGS: High-protein foods such as steak, pork, tofu

TIP: Feel free to change the leafy greens in this recipe depending upon what is available. Regular Swiss chard will work just as well as the red variety, and green kale is an acceptable substitute for purple.

PURE PECTIN

Pectin is a soluble dietary fiber found in varying degrees in all terrestrial plants. Some studies have concluded that the consumption of pectin can reduce blood cholesterol levels. In addition to the fiber this drink provides, you will receive 15 percent of your RDA of vitamin C with each serving.

Juice of 1 orange
1 very ripe persimmon, diced
1 Granny Smith apple, cored and coarsely chopped
1 red Bartlett pear, cored and coarsely chopped
6 cups still water

1. Place the orange juice in a blender. Add the persimmon, apple, and pear, along with 1 cup of the water. Puree on high speed until smooth, for about 2 minutes.
2. Strain through a fine-mesh sieve into a large pitcher, using a ladle to push most of the juice through as well. Add the remaining water, stir gently, and serve.

10 MINUTES   **8** SERVINGS

FOOD PAIRINGS: Fruit salads, omelets and other egg dishes, cookies such as shortbread or oatmeal

TIP: Underripe persimmons are extremely tart and unpalatable. Be sure to choose a very soft, ripe persimmon for this recipe.

SIMPLY BALMY

Lemon balm is a member of the mint family that aids digestion and can relieve nervous tension—who wouldn't want that to be an essential part of their day? Look for potted lemon balm plants at farmers' markets or ask a friend with a garden for a cutting. Much like mint, it is easy to grow and spreads rapidly. The lemon juice provides a hit of vitamin C.

1 tablespoon caraway seeds
¼ cup fresh lemon balm leaves (the tips are best)
Juice and zest of 1 lemon
6 cups still water

1. In a small, dry sauté pan, toast the caraway seeds lightly over medium heat for 2 to 3 minutes. Watch carefully to prevent burning.
2. Place the toasted seeds in a pestle along with the lemon balm and lemon zest. Grind lightly with the mortar and place in a sachet (page 14) or tea ball. Place the sachet in a large pitcher, add the lemon juice and water, and allow to steep in the refrigerator for at least 4 hours.
3. Remove the sachet and serve cold.

15
MINUTES
+
4 hours
to steep

6
SERVINGS

FOOD PAIRINGS: Consume as a digestif at the end of a meal.

TIP: Crush lemon balm leaves and rub them on your skin for a natural mosquito repellent.

WET/DRY

The ingredients are dry, and the water is wet. With a little time, a flavor exchange occurs that is sure to quench your thirst. Goji berries contain 18 amino acids, and cloves are known for their natural anti-inflammatory properties. Iron, vitamin C, and beta carotene are also in here. I have trouble keeping up with demand at my house for this addictive combination.

6 cups still water
2 tablespoons dried goji berries
2 tablespoons dried currants
2 tablespoons dried cherries
2 tablespoons dried cranberries
4 whole cloves, crushed

1. Heat the water to 100°F (check with an instant-read thermometer; it should feel barely warm to the touch). Pour into a bowl or jar, add the remaining ingredients, and steep at room temperature for 1 hour.
2. Cover and refrigerate for 8 hours.
3. Strain through a fine-mesh sieve into a pitcher and serve cold.

10 MINUTES
+
9 hours
to steep

6 SERVINGS

FOOD PAIRINGS:
Roasted meats, poultry, cheese

TIP: Save the rehydrated fruit for another use, such as a delicious addition to your favorite turkey stuffing recipe or blended with yogurt for a nutritious smoothie.

POMEGRANATE FLAIR

The combination of antioxidant-rich pomegranates and raspberries makes a refreshing beverage that is a perfect alternative to soda. Every pomegranate season (October to January), I buy a couple of extra pieces of fruit, remove all of the seeds, and freeze them. A little forethought guarantees I will have pomegranate seeds all year round.

10 fresh raspberries
¼ cup pomegranate juice
Juice of ½ lemon
4 cups chilled sparkling water
Ice cubes
¼ cup frozen pomegranate seeds (optional)

1. Place the raspberries and pomegranate juice in a glass measuring cup. Crush the raspberries very well with a muddler.
2. Strain the mixture through a fine-mesh sieve into a large pitcher, pressing on the solids with a ladle or rubber spatula to extract as much juice as possible. Add the lemon juice and water.
3. Serve over ice and garnish with the pomegranate seeds, if desired.

10 MINUTES

4 SERVINGS

FOOD PAIRINGS: Turkey burgers, salads, Middle Eastern food

TIP: To extract pomegranate seeds easily, immerse a halved fruit in a large bowl of water, then remove the seeds. Underwater, the seeds will stay intact and come out of the membrane more easily.

WIND-DOWN

Sleep is more important than most of us realize, and winding down at the end of a stressful day can be difficult at times. The ingredients in this water will naturally make the transition to rest easier—undoing many of the day's activities and providing one last opportunity for hydration before bed.

2 tablespoons fresh lavender leaves
5 fresh sage leaves
¼ cup dried chamomile flowers
3 tablespoons fresh peppermint leaves
4 whole cloves
6 cups still water

1. Bundle the lavender, sage, chamomile, peppermint, and cloves into a sachet (page 14) or tea ball.
2. Pour the water into a large pitcher. Add the sachet and steep in the refrigerator for at least 4 hours and up to overnight.
3. Remove the sachet and serve cold.

10 MINUTES
+
4 hours to steep

6 SERVINGS

FOOD PAIRINGS: Drink at the end of the day alone or with late-night snacks.

TIP: Chamomile flowers are most commonly found in the form of loose chamomile tea. If these are unavailable, use two chamomile tea bags; cut open the bags and proceed with the recipe.

Special Sippers

Throw out the soda. Forget about boring fruit juice. I guarantee you'll never want to drink those or plain water again after trying a few of the recipes in this chapter. Sure, some of the more exotic ingredients might take a little extra effort to find, and some of the techniques used are slightly more advanced, but the results are definitely worth it. Take a sip on the wild side!

Tomato Essence with
   Horseradish and Cucumber
Orange and Tamarind Elixir
Agua de Jamaica
Key Lime and Vanilla Spritzer
Pressed Watermelon
   with Basil Water
Herbes Sauvages

Thai Red Plum Fizz
Rain from Spain
Sangria de Agua
Tropical Fresh
Apio-Rey
Fruta Bomba
Mizu o Kudasai

TOMATO ESSENCE WITH HORSERADISH AND CUCUMBER

This is the Bloody Mary of waters (minus the vodka and excess calories, of course). A truly unique drinking experience awaits those with the patience to draw clear juices from red, ripe tomatoes and combine them with pristine water.

6 large, very ripe beefsteak tomatoes, quartered
2 tablespoons prepared horseradish
½ teaspoon sea salt
10 cracked peppercorns
1 teaspoon Worcestershire sauce
4 cups chilled still water
Juice from ½ lemon
1 recipe Cucumber Cubes (page 84)

20 MINUTES
+
2 hours to steep

6 SERVINGS

FOOD PAIRINGS: Egg dishes, red meat, grilled cheese sandwiches

TIP: For an extra kick, replace the prepared horseradish in this recipe with a 1-inch piece of peeled and grated fresh horseradish.

1. Puree the tomatoes, horseradish, salt, peppercorns, and Worcestershire sauce in a food processor.

2. Cut a 15-inch piece of cheesecloth and fold it in half to make a square. Place the square of cheesecloth in a large bowl and carefully pour the tomato puree into the center. Gather the corners of the cheesecloth and tie with a piece of kitchen twine.

3. Carefully lift the bag by the twine and suspend it above the bowl in the refrigerator by tying it to the handle of a wooden spoon. Rest the ends of the spoon on two stacks of cans to keep the cheesecloth above the surface of the liquid. Allow the juice to drain for at least 2 hours. Do not squeeze the bag or disturb it while draining, or the liquid will become cloudy.

4. Pour the water, lemon juice, and drained tomato water into a large pitcher, add the Cucumber Cubes, stir, and serve.

ORANGE AND TAMARIND ELIXIR

Tamarind provides a tart and quirky counter-point to the sweetness of the orange. Coriander seeds and cilantro leaves are two parts of the same plant, with two very distinct flavors. Both add an unexpected complexity to this unique drink.

¼ teaspoon coriander seeds
20 fresh cilantro leaves
Juice of 3 oranges
2 tablespoons tamarind paste
4 cups still water

1. Crush the coriander seeds with a mortar and pestle. Add the cilantro leaves and bruise them slightly.
2. Place the mixture in a large pitcher and add the orange juice, tamarind paste, and water. Stir well. Refrigerate for at least 2 hours and up to overnight.
3. Strain through a fine-mesh sieve into another large pitcher, and serve cold.

15
MINUTES
+
2 hours
to steep

4
SERVINGS

FOOD PAIRINGS:
Seafood,
Caribbean dishes,
Thai food

TIP: Tamarind is a tropical fruit cultivated in warm climates, and it is actually an ingredient in many familiar foods, including Worcestershire sauce. While fresh tamarind pods can be found in some markets, I find the paste to be easier to use (see the Resources section, page 93).

AGUA DE JAMAICA

Traditional *agua de Jamaica* is a Mexican infusion of dried hibiscus flowers and a lot of sugar. Skip the sugar and prepare this low-calorie, super-flavorful version before going to bed so that you can drink it the next day at lunch or dinner.

2 tablespoons dried hibiscus flowers
One 6-inch Mexican cinnamon stick, crumbled
4 cups still water
Juice of 1 tangerine

1. In a small saucepan, combine the hibiscus, cinnamon, and 1 cup of the water. Heat gently until the flowers begin to color the water, about 5 minutes.

2. Combine the mixture with the tangerine juice and the remaining water in a large pitcher. Refrigerate overnight.

3. The next morning, strain into another large pitcher, pressing on the solids with a ladle or rubber spatula to extract the most flavor. Serve cold.

10

MINUTES
+
overnight
to steep

4
SERVINGS

FOOD PAIRINGS: Tacos, roast pork, rotisserie chicken

TIP: *Flores de Jamaica* (dried hibiscus) and *canela* (cinnamon) are available at many Mexican grocers. Or check the Resources section (page 93) for online sources.

KEY LIME AND VANILLA SPRITZER

Key lime is the main ingredient here, balanced nicely with sweet vanilla and orange juice. Key limes are small, about an inch and a half in diameter, light yellowish green in color, and very tart in flavor.

1 vanilla bean, split lengthwise
¼ cup fresh Key lime juice
Juice of 1 orange, preferably Valencia
4 cups chilled sparkling water
Ice cubes

1. Scrape the tiny seeds from the center of the vanilla bean into a small bowl, then add the pods as well. Add the lime juice and orange juice to the bowl. Cover and steep in the refrigerator for at least 2 hours and up to overnight.

2. Strain the mixture through a fine-mesh sieve into a large pitcher. Add the sparkling water, stir gently, and serve over ice.

20
MINUTES
+
2 hours
to steep

4
SERVINGS

FOOD PAIRINGS: Cake, pie, and other desserts, as well as shellfish such as lobster, scallops, or shrimp

TIP: If fresh Key limes aren't available, you may substitute regular limes or bottled unsweetened Key lime juice.

PRESSED WATERMELON WITH BASIL WATER

Few things are more refreshing than watermelon. Pairing fresh watermelon juice with basil, sea salt, and a splash of vinegar makes a uniquely flavored water that you are sure to crave frequently.

4 cups watermelon chunks (about ¼ large melon)
6 to 8 large basil leaves
Pinch of sea salt
¼ teaspoon white wine vinegar
4 cups chilled still water

1. Combine the watermelon chunks and basil in a colander placed over a large bowl. Using a metal ladle or spoon, press the watermelon to extract as much juice as possible (the remaining pulp should be fairly dry).
2. Season the juice with the sea salt and vinegar and strain through a fine-mesh sieve into a large pitcher. Add the water, stir, and serve.

15 MINUTES

6 SERVINGS

FOOD PAIRINGS: Grilled chicken or fish, feta and tomato salad, shortbread cookies

TIP: Use yellow watermelon for an unexpected twist.

HERBES SAUVAGES

It may seem odd to use such strongly flavored herbs as rosemary and marjoram in an infused water—these are bold flavors most commonly reserved for savory dishes. But this is one delicious drink. Pair it with full-bodied meals that will stand up to this "meaty" beverage.

10 juniper berries
3 sprigs fresh rosemary
2 sprigs fresh marjoram
4 dried figs, coarsely chopped
Juice of 1 orange
6 cups still water

1. Crush the juniper berries in a mortar and pestle. Add the rosemary and marjoram and lightly bruise to release their flavor. Add the contents of the mortar and the fig pieces to a sachet (page 14) or tea ball.
2. Place the sachet in a large pitcher. Add the orange juice and water, stir, and allow to steep in the refrigerator for at least 6 hours and up to 12 hours.
3. Remove the sachet, stir gently, and serve.

10
MINUTES
+
6 hours
to steep

6
SERVINGS

FOOD PAIRINGS: Steak, lamb, roast pork

TIP: Add five 1-inch-long pine branch tips to the sachet in step 1 for another flavor element. The pine flavor adds a clean, mountain freshness to this water.

THAI RED PLUM FIZZ

This water cocktail features Balinese long peppers, which are known for their subtle nutmeg and citrus notes. Red plums add sweetness, and star anise and kaffir lime round out the flavor of this exotic beverage.

6 ripe red plums, halved and pitted
1 cup still water
1 star anise
2 Balinese long peppers
1 kaffir lime leaf
4 cups chilled sparkling water

1. Place the plums in a blender. Add the still water, star anise, peppers, and kaffir lime and puree well, for about 1 minute. Strain through a fine-mesh sieve into a large pitcher.
2. Add the sparkling water, stir gently, and serve.

10 MINUTES

4 SERVINGS

FOOD PAIRINGS: Spicy food, stir-fries, eggs

TIP: Check the Resources section (page 93) for where to buy Balinese long peppers and kaffir lime leaves. You might also look in Asian markets in your area.

RAIN FROM SPAIN

A Spanish staple, saffron, is the star here. Saffron is heralded as the world's most expensive spice as it must be painstakingly harvested from crocus flowers by hand. Don't worry, as we'll only be using a few cents' worth for this recipe.

6 cups still water
½ teaspoon saffron threads, crushed
½ bulb fresh fennel, trimmed and thinly sliced
Juice of 2 oranges, preferably blood or Valencia

1. In a small pan, heat ¼ cup of the water with the saffron until lightly simmering (about 3 minutes). Remove from the heat and pour into a large pitcher.
2. Add the fennel slices, orange juice, and the remaining water, stir, and allow to infuse in the refrigerator for at least 6 hours and up to 12 hours.
3. With a slotted spoon, remove the fennel, stir gently, and serve.

15
MINUTES
+
6 hours
to steep

6
SERVINGS

FOOD PAIRINGS: Paella, tapas, Mediterranean seafood

TIP: Save the green stalks of the fennel for use in Charentais Melon and Fennel Cubes (page 88).

SANGRIA DE AGUA

Okay, so this is not traditional Spanish sangria—that doesn't mean that it can't be just as satisfying. Red wine contains about 100 calories per glass; throw in some fruit, sugar, and brandy, and your diet is headed in the wrong direction fast. This version does without added sugar and alcohol, and has just a lightly sweet fruit flavor.

½ cup seedless red grapes
½ cup fresh cherries, pits and stems removed
Juice of 1 orange, preferably blood or Valencia
¼ cup pomegranate juice
Juice of ½ lemon
4 cups still water
1 recipe Grape Cubes (page 83)

1. Place the grapes and cherries in a food processor and pulse until broken up, 8 or 10 times. Transfer the chopped fruit to a large pitcher and add the orange juice, pomegranate juice, lemon juice, and water. Allow to steep in the refrigerator overnight.
2. Strain through a fine-mesh sieve into another large pitcher. Serve over Grape Cubes.

30 MINUTES
+
overnight
to steep

6 SERVINGS

FOOD PAIRINGS:
Chorizo, paella, grilled fish

TIP: Substitute frozen unsweetened cherries when fresh are unavailable.

TROPICAL FRESH

Exotic tropical flavors combine to transport you to another hemisphere. Be sure your passion fruit are shriveled and wrinkly before using—they are at their peak of ripeness when they look the worst. Passion fruit contains high levels of potassium, almost equal to that of bananas.

2 ripe passion fruit, halved
½ cup diced ripe mango
Juice of 1 lime
One 1-inch piece unpeeled fresh ginger, grated
4 cups still water

1. Scrape the seeds and pulp from the passion fruit into a food processor. Add the mango, lime juice, and ginger; pulse about 10 times. Pour the mixture into a large pitcher and add the water. Allow to steep in the refrigerator overnight.
2. Strain through a fine-mesh sieve into another large pitcher. Serve cold.

10 MINUTES
+ overnight to steep

4 SERVINGS

FOOD PAIRINGS: Pastries, shellfish, grilled poultry

TIP: The skin color of most mangoes is not a reliable indication of ripeness—a mango with an entirely green skin can be just as ripe as one with red or yellow markings. A ripe mango is slightly soft to the touch and has a sweet, floral scent.

APIO-REY

Inspired by Dr. Brown's Cel-Ray soda, the sparkling soda made with celery that was a favorite in my youth, I give you this reduced-calorie version, which can be made in the comfort of your own kitchen.

2 large stalks celery, coarsely chopped
1 teaspoon celery seeds
¼ teaspoon coriander seeds
1 cup seedless green grapes
1 cup still water
4 cups sparkling water

1. Puree the chopped celery, celery seeds, coriander seeds, and grapes in a blender with the still water. Strain through a fine-mesh sieve into a large pitcher.
2. Add the sparkling water, stir gently, and serve.

10 MINUTES

4 SERVINGS

FOOD PAIRINGS: Pastrami or corned beef on rye with deli mustard

TIP: Serve with Grape Cubes (page 83) for added fun.

FRUTA BOMBA

Fruta bomba is a Cuban term for papaya; it literally means "bomb fruit" due to the shape of the papaya and how they fall to earth from the trees. I was living in Miami the first time I heard someone use the words *fruta bomba* to describe this tropical treasure, and it still makes me smile whenever I hear it.

1 cup very ripe papaya chunks
Juice of 1 lime
Juice of 1 orange
3 large fresh mint leaves
6 cups still water
Ice cubes
Lime slices for garnish

1. In a blender, puree the papaya, lime and orange juices, mint, and 1 cup of the water. Strain through a fine-mesh sieve into a large pitcher.
2. Add the remaining water, stir, and chill, uncovered, for at least 2 hours and up to overnight. This essential chilling time allows the flavors to develop and the natural mustiness of the papaya to dissipate.
3. Serve over ice, garnished with thin slices of lime.

10 MINUTES
+
2 hours
to steep

6 SERVINGS

FOOD PAIRINGS: Roasted pork, ropa vieja (a Caribbean beef stew), Cuban sandwiches, and other Caribbean foods

TIP: Save the papaya seeds and use them as a natural meat tenderizer. Allow them to dry on a baking sheet, grind them with a mortar and pestle, and add them to marinades as needed.

MIZU O KUDASAI

Next time you go out for sushi, say "mizu o kudasai" to your waiter—it means "water, please." Just don't expect to get something this flavorful in your glass. Yuzu is a Japanese citrus fruit that recently has been cultivated in California—it looks like a small orange with mottled green and yellow skin. Substitute bottled yuzu juice when the fresh fruit eludes you.

4 fresh shiso leaves
One 2-inch piece fresh ginger, peeled and grated
Juice of 2 fresh yuzu, or ¼ cup bottled unsweetened
**   yuzu juice**
6 cups still water

1. Lightly crush the shiso leaves to release their flavor and place them and the ginger in a sachet (page 14) or tea ball. Place the sachet in a large pitcher and add the yuzu juice and water. Allow to infuse in the refrigerator for 4 hours, and up to 12 hours.
2. Remove the sachet, stir gently, and serve.

10 MINUTES
+
4 hours
to steep

6 SERVINGS

FOOD PAIRINGS:
Japanese food

TIP: Shiso is sometimes called Japanese basil due to its sweet, basil-like flavor. Look for it in Asian markets; it's also called oba or perilla.

Cubed Complements

Look beyond the liquid in the glass and consider the possibility that your ice cubes can be full of flavor as well. As they melt, the subtle flavor of these cubes slowly adds itself to whatever liquid you put them in, becoming more pronounced and more intriguing as you empty the glass. Be sure to use well-chilled water when making your cubes, as it will greatly reduce the time needed in the freezer.

Minty Cubes
Tangerine-Ginger Cubes
Grape Cubes
Cucumber Cubes
Orange Blossom and Vanilla Cubes
Cardamom–Green Apple Cubes
Strawberry-Kiwi Cubes
Charentais Melon and Fennel Cubes
Jamaican-Spiced Pineapple Cubes
Peach–Thai Basil Cubes

MINTY CUBES

Not only do these cubes taste great in practically any drink, the mint provides the added bonus of relieving tension headaches. I keep a bag of these cubes in my freezer for any time I need a little extra flavor, or pain relief, in my life.

1 small bunch fresh mint (¾ cup packed)
2 cups chilled still water

1. Remove the mint leaves from the stems and discard the stems.
2. Combine the water and mint in a blender and puree until smooth, for about 45 seconds. Pour the puree into standard ice cube trays and freeze.

10 MINUTES
+
2 hours
to freeze

28 ICE CUBES

WATER PAIRINGS: Sparkling Meyer Lemon Water, Cucumberade, Key Lime and Vanilla Spritzer

TIP: Peppermint or spearmint works equally well in this recipe, so use either or a mixture of both.

TANGERINE-GINGER CUBES

Tangerines were named for the first port city they were shipped to: Tangiers, Morocco. Today, prized for their easy-to-peel skin, they are grown around the world, including China, Spain, Brazil, and Japan. I employ only the juice here for its slightly sour sweetness.

One 1-inch piece fresh ginger, peeled and coarsely chopped
Juice of 2 tangerines
2 cups chilled still water

1. Place the ginger and tangerine juice in a blender with 1 cup of the water. Puree until smooth, for about 45 seconds.

2. Strain the puree through a fine-mesh sieve into a pitcher, pressing on the solids to extract as much juice as possible. Add the remaining water and stir to blend. Pour into standard ice cube trays and freeze.

15
MINUTES
+
2 hours
to freeze

28
ICE CUBES

WATER PAIRINGS: Pineapple and Lime Seltzer, Workout Fuel, Thai Red Plum Fizz

TIP: If tangerines are not available, substitute the juice of 2 clementines or the juice of 1 orange and ½ lemon.

GRAPE CUBES

I have to admit that this idea came to me while watching my young son drop grape halves into a glass of water. Since that day I have been watching him closely for further inspiration.

½ pound seedless red or green grapes
2 cups chilled still water

1. Cut the grapes in half and divide into two equal parts. Puree half of the grapes with ½ cup of the water in a blender until smooth, for about 30 seconds.

2. Pour the rest of the water into a pitcher. Strain the pureed grape mixture through a fine-mesh sieve into the pitcher, and stir well.

3. Place the remaining grape halves in the wells of standard ice cube trays. Fill the trays with the grape-water mixture and freeze.

15

28

MINUTES   ICE CUBES

+
2 hours
to freeze

WATER PAIRINGS:
Squirt of Citrus,
Wet/Dry, Apio-Rey

TIP: Be on the lookout for interesting seedless grapes. My favorite for this recipe is a new seedless Muscat—it has all the flavor of a regular Muscat grape without the bother of the seeds.

CUCUMBER CUBES

There is evidence that cucumbers have been cultivated for nearly 10,000 years. They originated in India and spread gradually throughout Europe before being brought to the New World by the Spaniards. Although it's doubtful that anyone made ice cubes from cucumbers until modern times, these relatives of watermelon and squash were a vital staple for the Egyptians, Romans, and Native Americans.

1 English cucumber, peeled, seeded, and coarsely chopped
Pinch of sea salt
2 cups chilled still water

Puree all of the ingredients in a blender until very smooth, for about 30 seconds. Pour the puree into standard ice cube trays and freeze.

10 MINUTES
+
2 hours
to freeze

28 ICE CUBES

WATER PAIRINGS: Thai Red Plum Fizz, Eau de Carotte, Tomato Essence with Horseradish and Cucumber

TIP: To quickly seed the cucumber in this recipe, cut it in half lengthwise and scrape the seeds out with the tip of a teaspoon. With a little practice, this can be done in one fluid motion.

ORANGE BLOSSOM AND VANILLA CUBES

While these cubes contain no sugar, the flavors of the orange blossom and vanilla lend a distinctly sweet note to everything you put them in.

1 vanilla bean, split lengthwise
2 cups chilled still water
2 tablespoons orange blossom water

1. Scrape the seeds from the center of the vanilla bean and place them and the pod in a small pan with ½ cup of the still water. Bring to a simmer over medium heat and allow to cook for 30 seconds, then turn off the heat and let cool to room temperature.

2. Place the orange blossom water and the remaining water in a pitcher. Strain the vanilla mixture through a fine-mesh sieve into the pitcher; stir well. Pour into standard ice cube trays and freeze.

10 MINUTES
+
2 hours
to freeze

28 ICE CUBES

WATER PAIRINGS: Honeydew-Mint Mist, Aloe-Asis, Rain from Spain

TIP: Look for orange blossom water in Asian or Middle Eastern markets. You can also find it online (see the Resources section, page 93).

CARDAMOM–GREEN APPLE CUBES

A member of the ginger family, green cardamom is most commonly used as a flavorful addition to coffee throughout the Middle East. Here it balances nicely with the sweet and tart notes of green apple.

3 green cardamom pods
1 Granny Smith apple, peeled, cored, and coarsely chopped
2 cups chilled still water

Puree all of the ingredients in a blender until smooth, for about 1 minute. Strain the liquid through a fine-mesh sieve into a pitcher. Pour into standard ice cube trays and freeze.

10 MINUTES
+
2 hours to freeze

28 ICE CUBES

WATER PAIRINGS: Crimson Dew, Pomegranate Flair, Orange and Tamarind Elixir

TIP: Double the recipe, skip the freezing step, and serve this as yet another flavored water. It's tasty enough to stand on its own.

STRAWBERRY-KIWI CUBES

Strawberry and kiwi are what can only be described as a classic modern combination. The two flavors just seem to go together—as if they were made for one another sometime during the mid-1980s. I love these cubes in plain water, preferably on a hot summer day.

10 strawberries, hulled and sliced
1 kiwi, peeled and sliced
Juice of ½ lemon
3 fresh mint leaves
2 cups chilled still water

Puree all of the ingredients in a blender until smooth, for about 2 minutes. Strain through a fine-mesh sieve into a pitcher, then pour into standard ice cube trays and freeze.

10
MINUTES
+
2 hours
to freeze

28
ICE CUBES

WATER PAIRINGS:
June Fields, Pure Pectin

TIP: Only in an act of strawberry desperation should you substitute frozen fruit for fresh in this recipe.

CHARENTAIS MELON AND FENNEL CUBES

Charentais melons are a variety of cantaloupe that were named after the French region of Charente. Look for them in specialty produce markets in late summer—they are smaller than cantaloupes, with ridges dividing the skin into regular segments.

½ ripe Charentais melon, peeled, seeded, and diced (about 2 cups)
¼ cup coarsely chopped fresh green fennel tops
Pinch of sea salt
2 cups chilled still water

Puree all of the ingredients in a blender until smooth, for about 2 minutes. Strain through a fine-mesh sieve into a pitcher, then pour into standard ice cube trays and freeze.

10 MINUTES
+
2 hours to freeze

28 ICE CUBES

WATER PAIRINGS:
Mora Picante, Simply Balmy, Pressed Watermelon with Basil Water

TIP: Use ¼ of a ripe cantaloupe instead of the Charentais melon in this recipe. The flavor won't be quite as refined, but it's an acceptable substitute.

JAMAICAN-SPICED PINEAPPLE CUBES

This drink features jerk seasoning, which comprises three main ingredients: Scotch bonnet peppers, allspice berries, and thyme. I find these three aromatic flavors, usually associated with savory meat dishes, to be a perfect match for tropical pineapple.

2 cups fresh diced pineapple
1 teaspoon jerk seasoning
Juice of 1 lime
2 cups chilled still water

Puree all of the ingredients in a blender until smooth, for about 2 minutes. Strain through a fine-mesh sieve into a pitcher, then pour into standard ice cube trays and freeze.

10 MINUTES
+
2 hours
to freeze

28 ICE CUBES

WATER PAIRINGS: Mango-Ginger "Beer," Agua de Jamaica, Fruta Bomba

TIP: Use dried jerk seasoning. The wet, jarred versions usually contain oil, an undesirable ingredient in ice cubes.

PEACH–THAI BASIL CUBES

Thai basil is a cultivar of sweet basil. Used to flavor a wide array of Thai and Vietnamese dishes, it is prized for its strong basil flavor and subtle licorice notes. Here it plays nicely with the floral sweetness of ripe peaches.

2 ripe peaches, pitted
2 fresh Thai basil leaves
Juice and zest of ½ lime
2 cups chilled still water

Puree all of the ingredients in a blender until smooth, for about 2 minutes. Strain through a fine-mesh sieve into a pitcher, then pour into standard ice cube trays and freeze.

10
MINUTES
+
2 hours
to freeze

28
ICE CUBES

WATER PAIRINGS: Sweet Tart, Lychee and Lime Water, Sangria de Agua

TIP: Look for fresh Thai basil in Asian markets, or check the Resources section (page 93) for an online source.

Eau de You

With a little experimentation, you are sure to make great-tasting designer drinks. Don't be discouraged if a few of your creations fail to please everyone. Just keep mixing until you get an exciting flavor profile that you like. Start out simply, mixing two or three ingredients your first few times. Once you get more experienced, you can get more creative. And don't forget to freeze some unique cubes to accompany your new masterpieces.

Use your imagination and the list below to invent your own flavor combinations.

FRUITS
apple
apricot
blackberry
blood orange
blueberry
cactus pear
cantaloupe
cherimoya
cherry
cranberry
golden kiwi
gooseberry
grapefruit
green kiwi
guava
honeydew
Key lime
lemon
lychee
mango
Meyer lemon
nectarine
papaya
passion fruit
peach
pear
persimmon
pineapple
plum
pomegranate
raspberry
seedless grapes
sour orange
star fruit
strawberry
tangerine
watermelon

HERBS
basil
borage flowers
chive
cilantro
curry leaf
dill
lavender
lemon balm
marjoram
mint
oregano
parsley
rosemary
sage
sorrel
tarragon
thyme

SPICES
ancho chile powder
caraway seed
cardamom
cascabel or chipotle chile
    powder
celery seed
cinnamon, ground or stick
clove
coriander seed
dill seed
fennel seed
ginger, fresh or ground
juniper berry
mustard seed
nutmeg
pepper, black or white
saffron
sea salt
vanilla bean

VEGETABLES
beet
carrot
celery
celery root
chard, Swiss or red
cucumber
fresh fennel
kale
mushroom, dried
parsnip
radish
spinach
tomatillo
tomato

ZINGS
cherry, dried
cranberry, dried
cocoa powder
coconut water
currant
dried fig
galangal
green tea
hibiscus flower
horseradish
kaffir lime leaf
lemongrass
Mexican cinnamon
orange blossom water
pine branch tips
raisin
rose water
shiso
tamarind
Thai basil
Worcestershire sauce
yuzu

Resources

WATER FILTERING

www.amazon.com
Culligan water filtration
pitchers

www.aquasana.com
Aquasana countertop water
filters

www.multipureco.com
Multi-Pure countertop
water filters

www.purwater.com
PŪR water filtration pitchers
and faucet filters

www.shopbrita.com
Brita water filtration pitchers
and faucet filters

www.target.com
Doulton countertop water
filters

www.waterpik-store.com
Waterpik faucet filters

INGREDIENTS

www.kalustyans.com
Rose water, orange blossom
water, Spanish saffron,
green cardamom, goji
berries, jerk seasoning

www.mexgrocer.com
Tamarind paste, dried hibiscus
flowers, Mexican cinnamon

www.ranchodesantafe.net
Ancho chile powder

www.salttraders.com
Balinese long peppers

www.templeofthai.com
Thai basil, lemongrass, and
kaffir lime leaf

www.beanilla.com
Various types of vanilla bean

www.amazon.com
Yuzu juice and coconut water

COUNTERTOP SELTZER MACHINES

www.everpure.com
Everpure Exubera Sparkling
and Chilled Water
Appliance

www.sodaclubusa.com
Soda-Club Fountain Jet,
Edition 1, and Penguin
machines

SODA SIPHONS

www.isi-store.com
iSi bottles and CO_2 cylinders

www.target.com
Liss bottles and CO_2 cylinders

MEASUREMENT EQUIVALENTS

Please note that all conversions are approximate.

LIQUID CONVERSIONS

U.S.	IMPERIAL	METRIC
1 tsp		5 ml
1 tbs	½ fl oz	15 ml
2 tbs	1 fl oz	30 ml
3 tbs	1½ fl oz	45 ml
¼ cup	2 fl oz	60 ml
⅓ cup	2½ fl oz	75 ml
⅓ cup + 1 tbs	3 fl oz	90 ml
⅓ cup + 2 tbs	3½ fl oz	100 ml
½ cup	4 fl oz	120 ml
⅔ cup	5 fl oz	150 ml
¾ cup	6 fl oz	180 ml
¾ cup + 2 tbs	7 fl oz	200 ml
1 cup	8 fl oz	240 ml
1 cup + 2 tbs	9 fl oz	275 ml
1¼ cups	10 fl oz	300 ml
1⅓ cups	11 fl oz	325 ml
1½ cups	12 fl oz	350 ml
1⅔ cups	13 fl oz	375 ml
1¾ cups	14 fl oz	400 ml
1¾ cups + 2 tbs	15 fl oz	450 ml
2 cups (1 pint)	16 fl oz	475 ml
2½ cups	20 fl oz	600 ml
3 cups	24 fl oz	720 ml
4 cups (1 quart)	32 fl oz	945 ml
		(1,000 ml is 1 liter)

Index

Note: *Italicized* page numbers refer to photographs.

Agua de Jamaica, 64
Aloe-Asis, 48
Antioxidant Power, 46, *47*
Apio-Rey, *74*, 75
Apple(s)
    Eau de Carotte, *42*, 43
    Green, –Cardamom Cubes, 86
    Pure Pectin, 52
    Sweet Tart, *30*, 31

Basil, Thai, –Peach Cubes, 91
Basil Water, Pressed Watermelon with, *66*, 67
Berries
    Antioxidant Power, 46, *47*
    Blueberry Twist, 26, *27*
    June Fields, 36
    Mora Picante, 34, *35*
    Pomegranate Flair, 56
    Strawberry-Kiwi Cubes, 87
    Sweet Tart, *30*, 31
    Wet/Dry, 54, *55*
Blueberry Twist, 26, *27*

Cardamom–Green Apple Cubes, 86
Carotte, Eau de, *42*, 43
Celery
    Apio-Rey, *74*, 75
Cherry(ies)
    Red, Spritzer, 28
    Sangria de Agua, 72
    Wet/Dry, 54, *55*
Coconut water
    Workout Fuel, 44
Cranberries
    Sweet Tart, *30*, 31
    Wet/Dry, 54, *55*
Crimson Dew, 29
Cucumberade, 45
Cucumber and Horseradish, Tomato Essence
    with, 60–61

Fennel
    and Charentais Melon Cubes, 88, *89*
    Rain from Spain, 70, *71*

Fruits. *See also* Berries; *specific fruits*
    Pure Pectin, 52
    washing, 17
Fruta Bomba, 76

Ginger
    "Beer," Mango, 37
    Eau de Carotte, *42*, 43
    Mizu o Kudasai, 77
    -Tangerine Cubes, 81
    Tropical Fresh, 73
    Workout Fuel, 44
Grape(s)
    Antioxidant Power, 46, *47*
    Apio-Rey, *74*, 75
    Cubes, *82*, 83
    Sangria de Agua, 72

Herb(s)
    Green, Infusion, 40, *41*
    Herbes Sauvages, 68
    washing, 17
    Wind-Down, 57
Honeydew-Mint Mist, 22, *23*
Horseradish and Cucumber, Tomato Essence
    with, 60–61

Ice cubes
    Cardamom–Green Apple, 86
    Charentais Melon and Fennel, 88, *89*
    Grape, *82*, 83
    Jamaican-Spiced Pineapple, 90
    making ahead, 16–17
    Minty, 80
    Orange Blossom and Vanilla, 85
    Peach–Thai Basil, 91
    Strawberry-Kiwi, 87
    Tangerine-Ginger, 81
Inner Earth, 49

Jamaican-Spiced Pineapple Cubes, 90
June Fields, 36

Kiwi-Strawberry Cubes, 87

Lemon balm
  Simply Balmy, 53
Lemon(s)
  Blueberry Twist, 26, *27*
  Cucumberade, 45
  Meyer, Sparkling Water, 24
  Rose Water with, 25
  Simply Balmy, 53
  Squirt of Citrus, 20
Lime(s)
  Cucumberade, 45
  Fruta Bomba, 76
  Key, and Vanilla Spritzer, 65
  and Lychee Water, 32
  and Pineapple Seltzer, 21
  Squirt of Citrus, 20
Liquid Iron, *50*, 51
Lychee and Lime Water, 32

Mango
  -Ginger "Beer," 37
  Tropical Fresh, 73
Melon
  Charentais, and Fennel Cubes, 88, *89*
  Honeydew-Mint Mist, 22, *23*
  Pressed Watermelon with Basil Water,
    66, 67
Mint
  Clean Spearmint Water, 33
  -Honeydew Mist, 22, *23*
  Minty Cubes, 80
Mizu o Kudasai, 77
Mora Picante, 34, *35*

Orange Blossom and Vanilla Cubes, 85
Orange(s)
  Crimson Dew, 29
  Fruta Bomba, 76
  Rain from Spain, 70, *71*
  Squirt of Citrus, 20
  and Tamarind Elixir, 62, *63*

Papaya
  Fruta Bomba, 76
Passion fruit
  Tropical Fresh, 73
Peach–Thai Basil Cubes, 91
Pineapple
  Cubes, Jamaican-Spiced, 90
  and Lime Seltzer, 21

Plum, Red, Fizz, Thai, 69
Pomegranate Flair, 56

Rain from Spain, 70, *71*
Rose Water with Lemon, 25

Saffron
  Rain from Spain, 70, *71*
Sangria de Agua, 72
Sparkling water, 11–13
Still water, 9–10
Strawberry(ies)
  June Fields, 36
  -Kiwi Cubes, 87
Sweet Tart, *30*, 31

Tamarind and Orange Elixir, 62, *63*
Tangerine(s)
  Agua de Jamaica, 64
  -Ginger Cubes, 81
Thai Red Plum Fizz, 69
Tomato Essence with Horseradish and
    Cucumber, 60–61
Tools
  blender, 15
  food processor, 15
  mortar and pestle, 15
  muddler, 15–16
  pitchers and stir rods, 16
  sachet, 14
  sieve, 13–14
  tea ball, 14
Tropical Fresh, 73

Vanilla and Key Lime Spritzer, 65
Vanilla and Orange Blossom Cubes, 85
Vegetables. *See also specific vegetables*
  Inner Earth, 49
  Liquid Iron, *50*, 51
  washing, 17

Water, for recipes, 9–13
Watermelon, Pressed, with Basil Water, *66*, 67
Wet/Dry, 54, *55*
Wind-Down, 57
Workout Fuel, 44

Yuzu
  Mizu o Kudasai, 77

About the Authors

Brian Preston-Campbell is a professional food stylist and former chef. A graduate of the Culinary Institute of America, he has brought his talent for food styling to national ad campaigns for such companies as Starbucks, Absolut, Nestlé, Godiva, and Smucker's. His creative food styling has also appeared in magazines such as *O: The Oprah Magazine*, *The New York Times Magazine*, *Prevention*, and *Men's Health*. In addition, he was the food stylist for several books, including *The Sneaky Chef* and *Good Spirits*, winner of an IACP Cookbook Award for Food Photography and Styling. He lives in New York with his wife and two children.

LYNDA PECKHAM

Jerry Errico is a food and advertising photographer and director whose clients include Goya, Kraft Foods, Bear Naked, Absolut, and the Culinary Institute of America. He was the photographer for a number of cookbooks, including *Cheese Hors d'Oeuvres*, *The Sneaky Chef*, *Quick and Kosher*, and *The Great American Grilling Book*. He lives and works in New York.